Essential Knowledge for Acrylic Painting Beginners

Written By:
SAMANTHA COUSTE

Copyright © 2022 by Samantha Couste

All rights reserved. No part of this publication may be reproduced, distributed, or transmitted in any form or by any means, including photocopying, recording, or other electronic or mechanical methods, without the prior written permission of the publisher, except in the case of brief quotations embodied in critical reviews and certain other noncommercial uses permitted by copyright law.

Book Design by HMDpublishing

I dedicate this guidebook to Michel. I'm forever grateful to you for your love and endless support. It has made all the difference!

CONTENTS

Introduction 5
Why Acrylic Painting? 6
How Long Will It Take to Learn How to Paint? 7
How to Join Acrylic Arts Academy to Level Up Your Skills 8
What Do I Need to Begin Acrylic Painting? 10
How to Set up Your Creative Space 14
All About Brushes 18
Types of Acrylic Paint Available & Their Qualities 23
How to Paint on Paper 27
Essential Art Terms 29
Creative Exercise to Understand Techniques and Materials 43
Stages of Creating an Acrylic Painting 47
How to Sketch on a Canvas: 49
When to Let Paint Dry 51
Basics of Color 52
How to Save Your Paint From Drying Out 60
How to Add Highlight and Shadow, Light Source 62
How to Measure & Paint Anything 63
Tips for Painting Fine Details 65
How to Remove Excess Paint 67
How to Varnish an Acrylic Painting 68
How to Store Your Canvas 70
Ways to Change the Nature of Acrylic Paint Using Additives ... 71
How to Join Acrylic Arts Academy's Helpful Artist Communities 73

INTRODUCTION

Hello, reader; I'm Samantha Couste. I created Acrylic Arts Academy and have been a painter since my youth. Art has always been important to me, and what I'll teach you here has been informed by my wealth of experience as an artist and instructor. Acrylic Arts Academy and its educational materials will be a fantastic supplement to what you'll learn in this book, so please take a moment to visit our website, acrylicartsacademy.com, and see what we have to offer.

Acrylic painting is fantastic, and this book is your complete guide. This is for those who feel compelled to paint but need help figuring out how to start. In this text, I'll give you all the tools you need to learn how to paint and advance yourself. All this is true without needing to attend art school or take expensive classes. Each section will teach you an essential skill to build your ability to paint and tap into your creativity. My goal is to give you the information you need to get started without overwhelming you with minutia. I have carefully curated this guidebook to get you painting with essential art concepts that will help you succeed. I formulated the information through my own experience and formal education.

So, this helpful guidebook is for you if you want to learn how to paint in acrylic. Art is essential, and your contribution is significant.

WHY ACRYLIC PAINTING?

First, I'd like to explain why acrylic paint may be preferable to oil, watercolor, or other media. But, of course, the answer to this question is a matter of opinion. So, let's look over the pros and cons of acrylic so that you can decide what type of paint might be best for you.

Acrylic painting is terrific and affordable fun. Acrylic paints cost less per ounce than oil and do not require additives to perform. They are economically priced and widely available from discount stores to specialty art shops. Compared to oil paint, acrylic is non-toxic, does not require ventilation, and cleans up easily with water.

This paint dries quickly in about 15 minutes, although it can take longer if you work with particularly thick paint textures. Amazingly, nothing needs to be added to the color to make it work. Likewise, no solvents are required to clean up afterward for your tools or workspace when using acrylic. Water is the only thing needed to clean paintbrushes; this paint cleans up easily unless it is dried.

I love the versatility of acrylic over watercolor and oil paint. This medium can create intricate hand-painted masterpieces, delightfully textured impasto art, and fluid artwork via acrylic pouring. Acrylic paint transforms to meet several needs by adding gels and mediums. These additives help paint act differently on the canvas according to your needs for any project. Mixing or changing the finish of artwork with these unique mediums is possible. Even though it hasn't been around for quite as long as egg tempera or oil paint, acrylic paint is known to be archival. Your painting will look great for years with proper care and appropriate storage.

HOW LONG WILL IT TAKE TO LEARN HOW TO PAINT?

The short answer to this question is that it depends solely on you. How much time can you devote to this new hobby, and how interested are you in learning to paint? Everyone is different; some folks could learn the basics within a month of intense instruction, or in six months with once-weekly lessons. Your drive and willingness to learn will set the timeline for your growth. Remember that even though you can learn the basics of painting in the timeframe mentioned above, mastery of any skill can take several years or a lifetime. It's also good to remember that you don't need to be a master of painting to enjoy it immensely.

We should make a pact with ourselves before taking on a new hobby, and that pact is: Don't give up when it becomes problematic. Being an artist will present challenges at times. Unfortunately, there's no rulebook to being a painter or schedule to keep you on track. However, knowing yourself and your tendencies will help you have the foresight to see past temporary hurdles you may encounter. So, please don't sell yourself short. An arts degree is not required to enjoy or succeed in painting. And it's never too late to start!

HOW TO JOIN ACRYLIC ARTS ACADEMY TO LEVEL UP YOUR SKILLS

This section will help you understand where to start as a beginner with us.

Acrylic Arts Academy's YouTube channel will teach you the essential skills to start painting with acrylic. Even if you haven't picked up a paintbrush before, we can help! First, we suggest you get the free printable guides that will teach you about the supplies you'll need to begin painting. A companion guide will quickly teach you what each of the most common paintbrush types can achieve. These printable guides are sent to you for free within 15 minutes of signing up at acrylicartsacademy.com/freeguides.

Within the first email you receive, there will be a helpful explanation of the essential supplies needed to begin painting. We have also included our best recommendations for each item and where to get them. This simple email will kick-start your painting journey! Next, it's best to subscribe to our channel and hit the bell icon to enable notifications of our newest acrylic painting videos. This simple act will inform you about upcoming tutorials and those that are readily available. I create new tutorials to help you paint each week and release them on Wednesday mornings.

When you get to the channel, check out the "Basics of Acrylic Painting - Total Beginners Start Here" playlist, which will teach you the basics of painting. Watch each video as this list has been carefully curated for beginners like you to learn the basics before you begin and through your first painting projects. From there, enjoy any of our step-by-step tutorials and curated playlists to begin your painting journey. It's just that easy! Get started today by visiting acrylicartsacademy.com/freeguides, and we will send you two printable guides and our best product recommendations for beginners.

WHAT DO I NEED TO BEGIN ACRYLIC PAINTING?

In this section, I'll explain the essential items for painting with acrylic. Then, I'll discuss why each is important and how it may help you in your creative practice as a painter. Supplies for acrylic vary slightly depending on your end goals. For instance, acrylic pouring requires a few different items versus paintbrush or palette knife-created artwork.

Acrylic paint is the essential material that we will need for this practice. Paint sells in various packaging and seemingly endless colors. The great thing about this is that you can either begin by purchasing the basic primary colors and mixing your hues, or you can buy each color you require pre-mixed. After that, it's entirely up to you. Mixing your shades of color is an excellent skill and will make things easier as you paint over time. This type of paint is available in varying kinds of finish, which means how shiny or dull the paint looks when dried. The type of finish with no shine is called matte. Next, there's satin, which has a very slight shine, moving on from there and getting progressively shinier. Gloss will have a moderate amount of sheen, and high gloss has the most. Finally, a metallic finish implies that the paint will look shimmery or glittery. Read the labels and be sure you're buying the acrylic paint you want. Oil paint and watercolor sell in similar-looking containers, and the difference between them matters.

Palettes are what we use to mix our paint colors. They come in various shapes and are usually made of plastic. Some palettes have shallow circular wells that hold paint hues separately, while others are flat and allow easy blending. There's even a type that keeps your paint from drying out, which features a tight locking lid—you can find it here. No matter your choice, any palette is usually inexpensive, easy to clean, and reusable. But, of course, you'll have to test to see which works best for you.

If you like to upcycle and recycle, here are some ideas for household items that work fine as a palette:

- Old ice trays
- Paper plates
- Old or scratched-up plastic plates
- Scrap cardboard covered with plastic wrap

You can store any palette inside a zippered plastic bag to keep it workable for longer between painting sessions.

A cup or jar is perfect for holding water that will clean your paintbrushes. Be sure to choose something sturdy that won't tip over easily. Old plastic cups and glass jars (from the fridge or otherwise) are easily found around the house and are a great way to recycle a previously used item.

We will, of course, require a set of tools with which to push the paint around. Paintbrushes are the apparent option, and they exist in many shapes and sizes. Each available brush shape helps artists add different features and elements to their artwork. These tools are essential for this practice in most cases. However, it is possible to paint without brushes or palette knives. Palette knives also come in many shapes and sizes and can be a perfect option for some painters. If you're going to get into acrylic pour painting, you may only use a palette knife for specific applications of color or to help mix different shades.

To ensure the cleanliness of your brushes, keep paper towels or old cloth towels handy. While you are working, you'll find that it's necessary to have a way to dry your brush off after swirling it in water. It helps to have a lighter-colored towel or cloth for this process so you can tell if the bristles have some of the previous colors stuck within them. It's imperative to preserve the boldness of your color palette and keep the water in the bristles from reaching your canvas. If the paint on your canvas has too much water, it may drip.

As painters, we need a surface to create images. Canvases are a popular and economical choice. Standard store-bought canvases are treated with gesso, which looks like thick white paint. It's then either stretched over a wooden frame and stapled or adhered directly to a panel. In the subsequent chapters, you'll learn much more about the different surfaces to paint on.

An easel helps prop up your canvas while you work. There are tons of different options here to meet many needs. In art stores and online, you'll find everything from small tabletop easels to large tripod easels that adjust quickly. There are even travel easels for those who want to paint en plein air (outside). Sometimes easels have a shelf or a small drawer to store tools in; others have a strap for traveling. Propping up your artwork will help you paint things more accurately and help you avoid a neck ache.

To preserve your current wardrobe and avoid a lot of heartaches, an apron will help keep your clothing paint-free. Taking the simple step of covering your clothes will help you immensely in the long run. Plus, specific aprons have pockets in the front that can easily house the next paintbrush you want or any other item you might need.

If you're choosing to work inside and are worried about making a mess, it's easy to use a drop cloth on the floor to keep things tidy. Anything from a couple of old towels, an old bed sheet, or plastic sheeting can be used as a drop cloth when working indoors. The idea is to create a barrier between your paint and the floor or carpet.

As your practice progresses, you'll find out which supplies are necessary according to personal preference. This list may grow as you adopt new styles and techniques.

HOW TO SET UP YOUR CREATIVE SPACE

Let's take a moment to talk about your creative space and where you'll be doing your painting. There are many ways to set up your creative space. I intend to give you the pros and cons of each setup so you can decide what's best for you moving forward. Remember that no matter how you choose to set up your creative space, it's essential to ensure it's ergonomically comfortable. Be aware of your body's positioning and do your best to sit or stand comfortably. You'll be glad you considered this as you begin to paint in longer sessions.

It's wise also to consider that no matter where you set up to paint, there's a possibility of making a healthy dose of 'mess.' Things such as paint splatters, accidental spills, and drops of paint falling on the floor are all possible. Rest assured that color cleans up relatively easily before it dries by simply using water, soap, and a towel. Acrylic paint is more challenging to remove when it's dry, so act fast if you have a spill.

There are ways to be careful and neat while painting, but that's not everyone's style, so be sure to protect your area (and its floors/walls) if you're particular about not getting paint anywhere.

If you're thinking about painting outdoors, please consider that it can be finicky, especially if you're working in an uncovered area. Besides fluctuations in weather hindering the practice altogether, one must also consider the humidity in the air as you work and let your paintings dry. The climate in your area may not be conducive to working outdoors, but it can help to have an outdoor space to spray your work with paint or varnish if needed. There are certain cases where it's vital to work in a well-ventilated setting, especially when using spray varnish or sealant.

As you consider the options for setting up your own studio space, consider where you're working and how you'd be most comfortable. Also, remember that many varying easels are available today, so please research the best option for you and your situation. In addition to the folded and tripod easels pictured below, there are desktop easels, very small or very large easels, and even travel-friendly easels at your disposal.

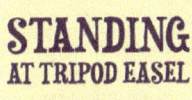

STANDING AT TRIPOD EASEL

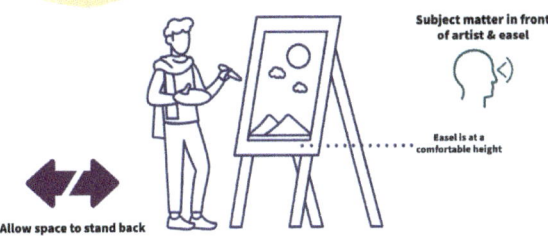

Using a tripod easel is the classic method for many art students in high school and beyond. However, some people prefer to stand while painting. To work this way, set up your easel as usual and adjust the height. Place your easel so that the bottom of your painting is around hip height or whatever is comfortable. This is essential if you're working with a large canvas. Placing your canvas any lower than hip height will result in stooping over uncomfortably.

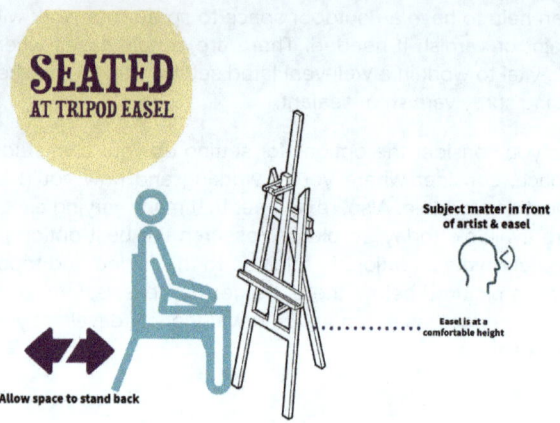

If working with a much smaller canvas, raise the lower frame of your easel as comfortably as possible. Make sure your arms and shoulders are at a comfortable angle, no matter where you have your canvas situated. Tripod easels can typically extend the legs and move the lower frame so that you can work with various-sized painting surfaces and adjust as needed. A good idea in this type of setup is to allow enough space for you to move back from your work from time to time. Be sure there's space behind you to do this, if possible.

Suppose the legs don't extend high enough for you to work while standing; working seated is an excellent second option. Set your easel to your left or right, depending on your dominant hand. Place the easel on the most comfortable side if you're painting objects or scenery right in front of you. This setup works well if you're using a screen like your tablet, laptop, or computer as a reference. This seated option is also ideal when using a bedside table or artist's desk.

If you have any physical limitations and are worried that these painting setups will not work for you, do not despair. Artists throughout history have figured out how to paint in particular circumstances, and you can too. Look up Frida Kahlo, for example, and you'll find that though she spent much of her life confined to bed while healing from various surgeries, she still found a way to paint! Therefore, I urge you not to give up and seek adaptive equipment to help you on your journey.

ALL ABOUT BRUSHES

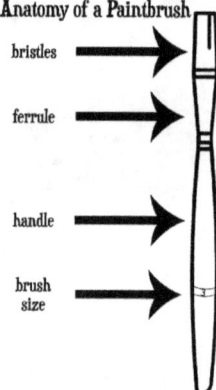

Anatomy of a Paintbrush
- bristles
- ferrule
- handle
- brush size

It's worthwhile to explain the anatomy of the painting implement that we'll use most often—the paintbrush. The simple design of the paintbrush hasn't changed much over history because it works!

So, let's talk about the components of a paintbrush:

First, there are the bristles. Paintbrush bristles can consist of varying materials; check the label of any brush you intend to buy to be sure it's suitable for acrylic paint. To ascertain this, find the writing on the brush's handle. It will say oil, watercolor, or acrylic. Nylon bristles seem to work best with acrylics, which is excellent news as they're economically priced and sold in multipacks.

Then, there's a handle usually made of wood or plastic. The number on the handle denotes the size and can help you choose the correct tool or easily replace a brush with its equivalent. Handles vary in length for different types of projects. Choose what best suits you and your work. I usually use a mix of longer handles for my larger brushes and shorter handles for my detail brushes. But, again, it's entirely up to you as the artist.

Next, there's a ferrule, which is the metal tubing that holds the handle and bristles together. This metal piece can be clamped or glued.

There are a few essential types of paintbrushes used in acrylic—an angled brush is excellent for creating crisp edges and straight lines. It can be helpful when painting long blades of grass, leaves, and other vegetation. In addition, this brush works well to add movement to water due to its ability to slice angled lines back and forth with ease. Overall, this is a versatile brush.

You can use a round brush to draw lines, create texture, or fill small areas. A round brush can make most things but will not quickly cover large areas or work for small details. The brush strokes created with this implement can vary depending on how you apply the paint. For example, a stamping motion may help create texture quickly; short wispy brush strokes will create slender lines that break apart at the tips. Depending on the size, you can use this for stippling art, writing text within your art, and more.

For tiny details and thin lines, use a liner brush. This brush is usually relatively small with fewer long bristles and is flexible. This brush will be essential when painting letters, calligraphy, or pinstripe-style designs.

Detailer brushes come in varying shapes and sell in a multi-pack. Each brush contains very few, typically short bristles. As a result, they're great for adding small details and flourishes to your artwork or miniature project.

A flat brush has square edges and multiple uses. It's a favorite for quick coverage and helps make lines or edges depending on the orientation in which you hold this implement. In addition, you can use the corners for detailing when the brush is tipped on its side and used with gentle pressure.

A filbert brush looks like a flat brush with a rounded tip. This brush style will serve you well if you like painting florals, natural vegetation, or trees.

A fan brush is perfect for making vegetation and adding texture. I also use this brush to create clouds and long grass blades. This brush is a versatile favorite, made even more famous by Bob Ross and his happy little trees.

A wash brush can also be called a large area brush because of its size. Use this paintbrush to fill large areas and create big swaths of color. You can also use a wash brush for texturizing and forming large areas of bushy vegetation.

These brushes all come in various sizes and are made from different materials. Be sure to buy brushes suitable for acrylic paint, the difference in materials matters to this practice.

● HOW TO CARE FOR BRUSHES:

There are a few skills in acrylic painting that are essential to know before you paint on canvas. One of those crucial skills is learning to clean up after you're through with artwork, including cleaning your paintbrushes. This method is easy, quick, and doesn't require harsh chemicals. My easy process will help to extend the life of your acrylic paintbrushes.

Follow these steps to clean your paintbrushes well without chemicals. First, cleaning up directly after you're finished painting is best. Try not to let your paintbrush dry with paint still on it; it's a pain to get the brush back to normal afterward, though it is possible. If you need a bit of time before cleaning up, it's better to temporarily leave your brushes in water. Be advised that letting brushes soak for too long can be problematic and weaken the structure of your paintbrush and its bristles, and you'll notice that the tips will bend in a "J" shape. Bent bristles are undesirable because they affect how the paintbrush applies pigment moving forward.

After painting, bring your tools to a sink or other water source. Remove any excess paint into a trashcan beforehand so you don't get color down the sink. You can also use paper towels to squeeze the paint off the bristles before washing them off. Another way to get the excess paint off the bristles is to swish the brush in your jar of water before swiping the brush back and forth on a paper towel. The idea is to get most of the paint off your paintbrush and into the trash versus down the drain.

When ready, let the brushes rinse under running water. Then, begin swirling your paintbrush lightly in the center of your palm under water. The circular motion helps draw out the paint to the ends of the bristles. Starting where the ferrule and bristles meet, use your index and middle fingers to remove excess water like a squeegee. Doing this will help you to reform the bristles of your brush quickly so they're flat across and look neat. Place your brushes on a towel to dry. Once they're pretty dry, store them with the handle side down or lying flat. Depending on how many paintbrushes you have, keep them in anything from a disused cup, glass jar, coffee mug, or basket. We recommend letting the paintbrushes dry out before storing them so that any leftover moisture in the bristles won't weaken the glue holding the handle, ferrule, and bristles together. This simple practice extends the life of your brushes and saves you money in the long term.

Please note that it's not incredibly kind to your home's plumbing to dump heavily tinted paint-laden water down the sink. As the name implies, acrylic paint contains plastic components that can seemingly build up in water pipes over time. If you're concerned about this problem, know that some people put their paint water in a bucket lined with a trash bag and a few inches of kitty litter in the bottom. This method presupposes that it's better to collect the water in something that goes in the trash rather than into the water system. Another approach is to add paint-tinted water in a good-sized bucket and let it sit (likely outside with some covering) until the water evaporates, leaving the paint particles at the bottom of the receptacle to throw away. Research a way to get rid of water like this and choose the best option for your particular situation.

If you mistakenly let your paintbrushes dry with paint on the bristles, soak them in rubbing alcohol for several hours or a day until the paint peels off the brush. Be sure to fill a jar or glass with rubbing alcohol until it covers the bristles—no further. If you soak the brush past the paint bristles, it may loosen the glue that holds the ferrule to the handle, making it wiggly. It may take a while, but rubbing alcohol should do the trick.

TYPES OF ACRYLIC PAINT AVAILABLE & THEIR QUALITIES

Let's chat about the different types of paint used in acrylic. Imagine visiting your local art store; as you find the paint aisle, you find jars, tubes in various sizes, bottles, and outright tubs of materials. Suddenly overwhelmed, you wonder which one is the best to use and how a person should know such a thing. This portion of the guide will demystify those questions and help you understand the different types of acrylic paint.

If you see large squeeze bottles of paint in primary colors, they are probably poster paints. This acrylic style is affordable but not necessarily high quality from a hobby painting perspective. Poster paints are often used in classroom and childcare settings or for making temporary signage, as the name implies. These paints have the consistency of mayonnaise, are less liquid than craft paint, and often lack pigment density.

Paint that comes in a tube or a jar can have more body to it and is thicker than craft paint. When we say that the color is thick, we mean it stands up more than craft paint. If you pour craft paint, it will be more like a puddle versus color in a tube, which would be more like the thickness of toothpaste. Further, acrylic paint can have more or less body, depending on the brand. Some pigments may already suit your needs due to their thickness. Our favorite paint is Liquitex Basics, for the value and quality it provides.

● WHAT DOES IMPASTO MEAN?

Impasto means that the acrylic paint you're using has a texture due to its thickness. Paint of this type gives a buildable structure to the pigment, which may be desirable to some painters. However, you'll need to add a heavy body gel or impasto medium to bulk up a color that isn't thick enough. Generally speaking, the impasto medium looks like a type of white paint.

To use impasto or heavy body medium, mix it into your paint and apply it as usual. Always refer to the label to know how much to add and how to best use that particular product. Though the gel may look like white paint, it will dry clear and not affect the color of your paint. Each medium has a specific type of finish, so pay attention to the label. For example, high gloss will be gleaming, whereas matte will have a dull finish, and there are several options in between.

When you add this type of medium to your paint, you may notice that the color is not quite as vivid as before, so it's essential to add the correct ratio of paint to the medium. If your paint has lost too much pigment after adding the gel medium, add more pigment to the balance. Further, acrylic paint can have more or less body, depending on the brand.

● DIFFERENT STYLES OF CANVAS

Regarding canvas, you, as the painter, have a few options. Each has its merits, and I would like to inform you of the benefits of either. After you read the section, you'll have a better idea of what you prefer; it will come down to personal preference.

Canvas is linen treated with gesso. Gesso is a heavy-body acrylic medium that seals off the porous nature of cloth, making it suitable for painting. People paint on canvas that is either stapled onto a wooden frame or adhered to a stiff cardboard panel. Either way, the canvas is treated the same before it's fixed to a structure or board.

Using a canvas panel is often an excellent choice for a beginner on a budget. Canvas panels consist of triple gesso primed canvas that's been stuck to a stiff cardboard panel. Though this is a thinner option, the style of the canvas is still sturdy and doesn't bend or flex. In addition, the canvas panel is about an eighth of an inch thick and can easily fit into most standard photo frames. This simple fact can help eliminate or significantly reduce professional framing costs, allowing you to easily hang your art in your home or give it as a gift.

If you anticipate doing acrylic pour painting, canvas panels won't be a good fit. Due to its delicate nature, the excess moisture from all that paint will inevitably make the panel bow. In addition, it's not always easy to flatten a panel without damaging or cracking paint. As with impasto painting, canvas panels would not be the best choice if you're using heavy body paint. In these instances, go with stretched and stapled canvas. The canvas panel is sold in affordable multipacks and is budget-friendly without sacrificing the quality of a canvas surface. This surface doesn't respond well to excessive moisture but is perfect for practicing techniques without breaking your budget.

Stretched and stapled canvas is also commonly sold in a multipack; many thicknesses are available from 1/4" to 2" gallery canvases. This canvas style comes in many sizes, some larger than a panel. Some stores will rate panels and stretched canvas, saying the thinner versions are only for kids or students. The fact is, the surface is not different, and it only matters what you prefer. When shopping in-store, take a moment to check over a prospective canvas or set of canvases that you're looking to purchase. There are minor dents occasionally occurring during shipping, and it's worth it to inspect anything you're about to buy in store.

Stretched and stapled canvas holds up to acrylic pour painting and several applied paint layers. You can also hang it up on the wall without a frame. If you want to frame a canvas like this on your own, purchasing a structure that's deep enough to accommodate its thickness is best. You can find frames suited for paintings on canvas online at retailers like Amazon and beyond. Look for 'frames for paintings' or 'shadow box frames"; you should be able to find something to suit your work. Another option is to bring your work to an art store and have the professionals frame it for you, where you'll be able to choose a specific frame in several styles and choose options like a mat board to act as a border around your painting inside of the frame. You can accent your work by choosing a color other than black or white mat board. Expect to pay a moderate amount for this service; remember that it's perfectly acceptable to work this cost into the final price tag for your work if you sell it.

HOW TO PAINT ON PAPER

I prefer to paint on canvas because it's sturdy and perfect for accepting paint. You can, however, use paper as your painting surface as well. Art paper may be cheaper than canvas in some instances and can easily be DIY framed.

To experience success in using acrylic paint on paper, make sure you use thick and heavy paperweight. A dense type of paper will help avoid curled-up or buckled edges and allow you to create lasting artwork.

To know if the paper will be thick enough for paint, pay attention to the sticker, label, or signage that describes the paper you're about to use. There will be a number with 'lb' or 'gsm' after it, denoting the paper's thickness and weight. Choose thick paper; for instance, 300 gsm or 140 lb weight would be appropriate. For reference, the paper you use in your printer or to write a letter is 20 lb-30 lb weight paper.

Art paper used for painting can be cold or hot-pressed. Hot and cold-pressed papers differ in the way they are created. Cold-pressed paper will have more texture than hot-pressed paper, which will be much smoother. That said, 300 gsm-350 gsm or 100 lb-140 lb paper would likely be the best bet for acrylic paint as it's much thicker and will stand up to multiple layers of paint. So, naturally, the higher the number that a paper is in pounds or grams, the thicker it is overall.

You can also get a visual on the paper surface you'd like to use and go from there. For example, card stock may be fine for light painting if you're making cards or crafts. If you're unsure whether your paper is thick enough, try the theory by painting a small patch of color on the paper you'd like to use and let it dry completely. If the paper buckles or curls up, it may be too thin to handle paint.

To avoid having the paper roll up, wrinkle, or otherwise change, tape the outer edge of your paper. This step will easily keep your paper flat while working, and effortlessly creates a clean, white border when you remove the tape. Be sure to use [painter's tape](#) or something similar so that you don't rip or harm the edges of your paper when removing the tape. There are products such as low-tack artists' tape, which are made specifically for this process. The adhesive is such that it won't damage your paper when you remove it. All the same, remove the tape from your painting surface with a slow and even pull. The risk of damage from adhesive occurring is higher with thick, fibrous cold-pressed papers. So be aware and research the reviews section for prospective products.

ESSENTIAL ART TERMS

Essential art terms are words and concepts necessary to know as a creative learner. The following section discusses the art concepts that will help you understand acrylic painting and start your artistic practice. This terminology will help you better comprehend art and painting.

LINE

Lines are the visual representation of a point moving through space. Lines can show direction and texture, portray a visual mood, and more. When you change the properties of lines, they can represent different meanings. For example, a thick delineation makes an image seem bold and creates a strong impact, whereas a thin marking can visually define something delicate or frail. Contour lines trace the outer edge of an object, revealing its two-dimensional shape. An organic form depicts a different feeling than a shape with sharp or jagged angles. Lines can be multiplied and layered, forming beautiful patterns. They can also show rhythm, like a heartbeat.

TEXTURE

American painter, John Sloan, once said:

"There is a better chance of getting an exciting painting from a labored study with texture than from a fine drawing without it."

So, what is texture in art? Texture in an artwork is the quality of a surface that light reveals. Meaning that if you could touch the surface, it would feel anywhere from flat to sharp, depending on the nature of the object. Without this vital art concept, everything we see would seem flat.

● PERSPECTIVE

When organizing shapes in space, perspective is essential. Simply put, perspective is your point of view for any image. It's how you see things from where you are. To paint an accurate perspective, your subject matter's height, width, and depth must be correct. The point of view from which you portray your subject will determine the size and shape of aspects of your art to demonstrate depth and distance. A change in perspective will mean a difference in the angle and shape of your subject matter so that your art relays a believable image in space. In summary, perspective is about the point of view and arranging shapes or objects in a way that makes sense to the person looking at your art.

As the artist, you control your art's perspective in some ways. The snapshot image you capture as a painting orients the viewer to your perspective in the visual world you've created. For instance, if you paint a field of sunflowers from the perspective of a person, the flowers might be a little lower than eye level, and the middle ground would expand upward to the horizon line, which would anchor the skyscape. The perspective would change drastically if the outlook were from a bird's eye view, from the air, and directly above. We would observe the entirety of the field as a flat square filled with flowers. There wouldn't be a semblance of a foreground, middle ground, or background. If the perspective was such that we had a small animal's point of view, our scene would be made up of towering flowers and stems without much background or a skyscape to be seen. The perspective of artwork varies by the angle its observers view things.

FORESHORTENING

With perspective in mind, you'll see foreshortening as a crucial part of your process.

Let's say you're painting a portrait where the person is pointing straight ahead, right at you. To portray the arm, hand, and fingers, you would need to utilize foreshortening. Foreshortening changes how you paint a subject matter pointed at the viewer. Foreshortening works by allowing objects to make visual sense to the observer of your art. Foreshortening is a classic case of painting what you see and not what you know, which is the illusion of this art concept.

Notice how the space on the left, highlighted in red, represents the distance between the top of her shoulder and elbow. It's an almost unbelievably small space, which shows foreshortening in action. The area on the right, highlighted in blue, represents the distance from her elbow to her fingertips. It would help if you reduced the length and angle of the hand from the shoulder to portray an accurate perspective in this example image. Without foreshortening and perspective, the illusion of depth could not exist on a flat surface.

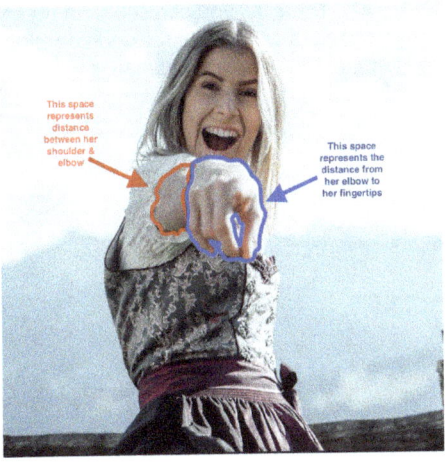

• PROPORTION

Proportion means that any objects in an artwork are sizes that make sense to one another. Proportion is the size of things that makes spatial sense. An example of something proportional is the size of a dog's paw versus the rest of the dog. A dog's paw is neither too large nor too small—it is simply the size that makes sense and is proportionate to its body.

Another way to consider this art concept is to think of the pieces on a chessboard. Chess pieces vary slightly in height and design but are proportionate to each other regarding their size. Therefore, as a group, their respective sizes make sense together.

• SCALE

For a viewer to best enjoy your art, you'll want to make sure you've got a solid understanding of proportion and scale. Scale is the perceived size of the objects or space inside your artwork. For example, the scale of a painting featuring a hilly landscape is more significant than that of a painting depicting a vase of flowers; as you can see from these two examples, scale changes with the perceived size of the space or objects represented in an artwork.

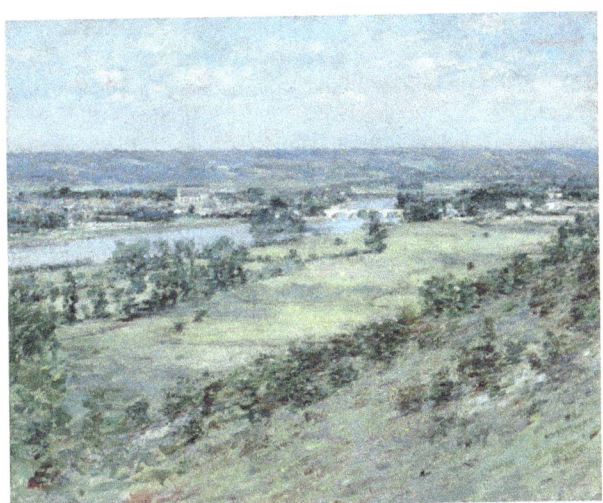

Theodore Robinson, "The Valley of the Seine, from the Hills of Giverny" c.1892

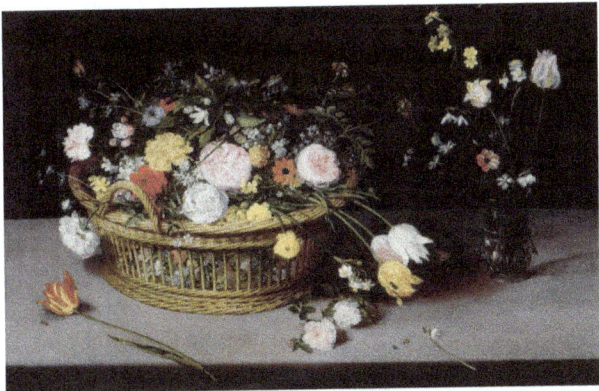

Jan Brueghel the Elder, "Flowers in a Basket and a Vase", c. 1615.

• COLOR

Color is the general term that covers every hue and shade of the light spectrum as we see it with our eyes. The colors red, orange, yellow, green, blue, indigo, and violet make up the rainbow. The primary colors are red, yellow, and blue. The secondary colors are green, orange, and purple. This equation creates tertiary colors—add one primary color to one secondary color, and you'll arrive at a tertiary color. Examples of tertiary colors include red, orange, blue, purple, blue-green, red-purple, yellow-orange, and yellow-green. Complementary colors are directly across from one another on the color wheel and suit one another nicely. Learn much more about this important term and concept in The Color Chapter.

• COMPOSITION

Composition is the arrangement or placement of elements within a work of art. For example, colored pencils are arranged in this simple photo to show their form in space. The composition shows the yellow pencil next to the orange, all in a pattern.

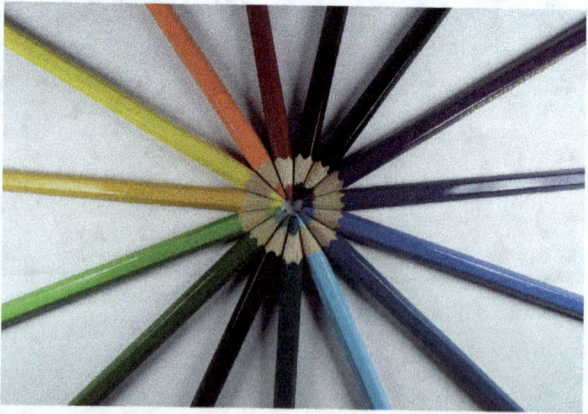

SPACE

Space denotes the area within, around, above, or below an object or objects within the visual plane. Positive space is the area occupied by the things in a work of art. Negative space is the area between the primary objects in a work of art.

Let's consider this artwork from history to help us understand the concept of space:

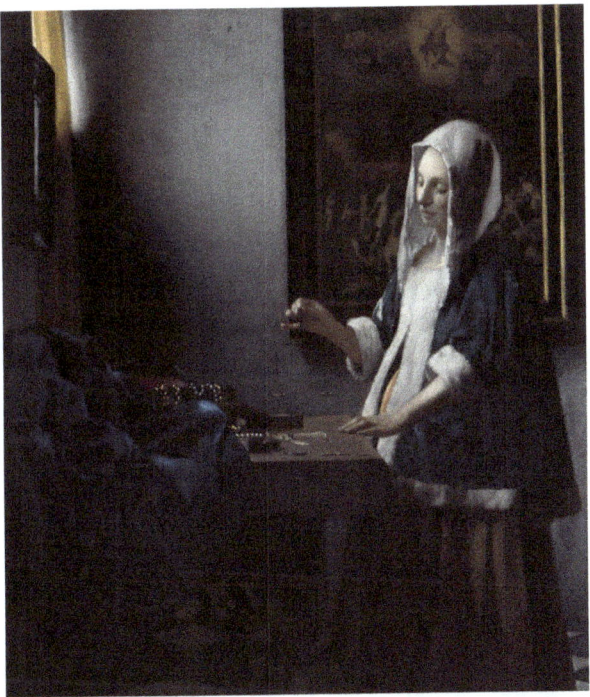

Johannes Vermeer, "Woman Holding a Balance", c. 1664

The composition in this painting is such that the visual weight is mainly on the right side, with the female figure painting on the wall, table, and drapery as the positive space. The negative space is located around the central subjects and is represented here mainly by the blank wall in the background.

● TECHNIQUE

The technique is how you create your artwork. If you're a painter, your technique may be using a paintbrush on a stretched canvas. It may also mean mixing your paint with medium and pouring it over the canvas. The materials are similar, but the technique is different. The technique can also indicate how you apply your paint to the canvas and which tools you use to complete this task. There's a technique involved whether you're using a cup filled with color, a traditional paintbrush, a palette knife, or a spray can. The idea of technique can go even further to describe how an artist layers paint, uses color in juxtaposition with other shades, or explains how one applies the paint to a surface. As artists and humans, we learn more as time progresses, implying that your technique will likely change and improve as you learn.

● MATERIALS

Materials are the specific items you'll need to make the art you're imagining. Since the technique is how you create your art, materials help make that technique happen. For instance, if you want to create an acrylic painting, your materials would be a canvas, paint, paintbrushes, varnish, and anything else used to create the finished product. Materials and techniques are the backbone of your creative process and may evolve as your interests and skills grow.

● FOREGROUND

We artists create illusions whenever we paint a 3D object on a flat surface. A good understanding of foreground and background is essential to achieve a believable depth in space. Understanding foreground and background helps artists create a sense of realism in their work.

Let's consider this painting from art history:

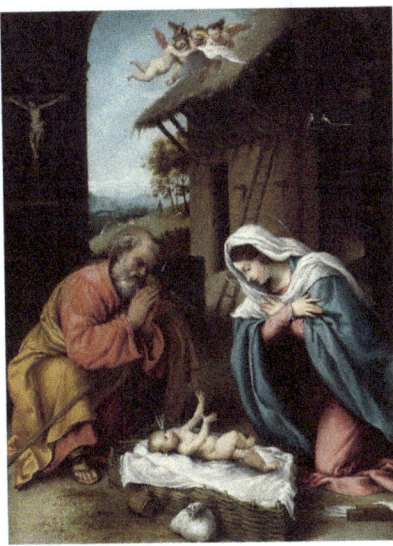

Lorenzo Lotto, The Nativity, 1523. Oil on panel.
(This image is in the public domain.)

The foreground of a painting appears first in the frame and is closest to the viewer. For example, the foreground in this painting appears in the lower half of the frame. These objects appear more prominent because they are closer. The brighter colors and enhanced contrast in their hair, skin, and clothes also help to bring the imagery forward in our frame of view.

The background appears in the upper half of this image. Notice how the objects in the distance are darker, less detailed, and smaller than those in the foreground.

Finding the foreground isn't always as simple as splitting the canvas in half at the horizon line, though.

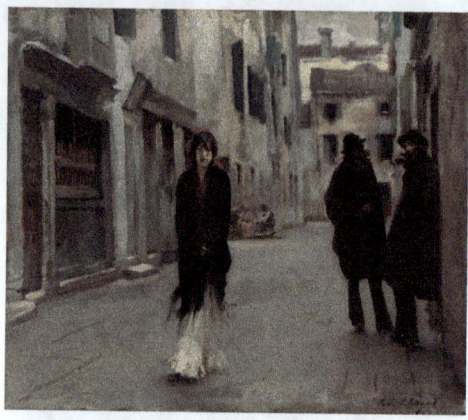

If you half this painting diagonally, the foreground and background can be recognized. Here, we can see that the foreground is on the left and the background is on the right.

John Singer Sargent Street in Venice, 1882. Oil on Wood. (This image is in the public domain.)

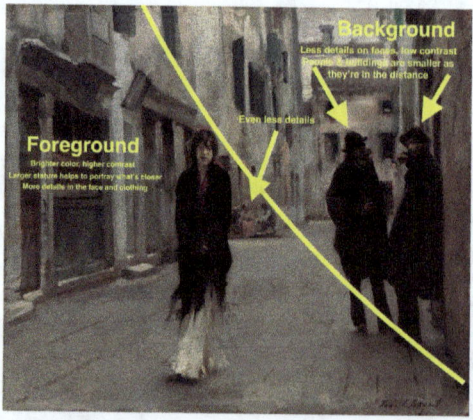

On the left side, the foreground begins at the top of the female's head and extends to the lower-left corner. It's good to note that the foreground features brighter colors and higher contrast as the difference between light and dark varies more with the colors in the background. The woman on the left has a larger stature than the other figures in this painting, which helps to visually portray that she is closer to us in the foreground of this frame. In general, we can see that there are more details included on her face and clothing. Because she is closer to the viewer, these details are apparent. In addition, she is more focused than the rest of the painting. All these factors together help to create a depth of space between the front and back of the frame.

BACKGROUND

The background of a painting represents what is further off in the distance. How much we see in the background depends on the angle of view. As we can see in this John Singer Sargent artwork, sometimes the background isn't simply the top half of an image. The background in this painting is located to the right and includes several figures, a roadway, and buildings. Notice how the objects in the distance are darker, less detailed, and smaller than those in the foreground. In this painting, we can notice that the people in the background have fewer details on their faces and clothing and a lower contrast overall. The third set of people in the back have even fewer details than the two gentlemen in the middle.

To summarize, the foreground represents objects and the space closest to the viewer.

Conversely, the background implies things or scenery farthest from the viewer.

● BALANCE AND SYMMETRY

If a picture is nicely balanced, the visual weight of the image is spread somewhat evenly across the canvas. Balance means that there's equal subject matter across your field of imagery. It implies that the subject matter is either centric or evened out by some other visual aspect.

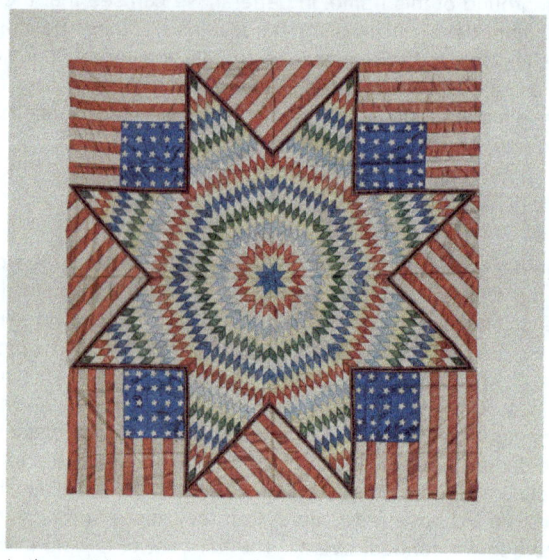

Let's consider this image by Fred Hassebrock, created in 1941.

In this example, the image is centric and balanced. There's also equal symmetry, which means that if you divide this image in half, both sides would be identical. If something is asymmetrical, the visual weight is greater on one side, leaving the impression unbalanced.

Giovanni Battista Moroni, "Titian's Schoolmaster," c. 1575.

This painting illustrates an excellent example of what we mean by asymmetry. It's by [Giovanni Battista Moroni](), titled ["Titian's Schoolmaster,"]() created in 1575. The solitary figure in this artwork is leaning in his chair on the right side of the frame. Because the space on the left is empty, this image is asymmetrical. If something was on the left, the painting would have more balance but wouldn't be symmetrical as both sides wouldn't mirror one another.

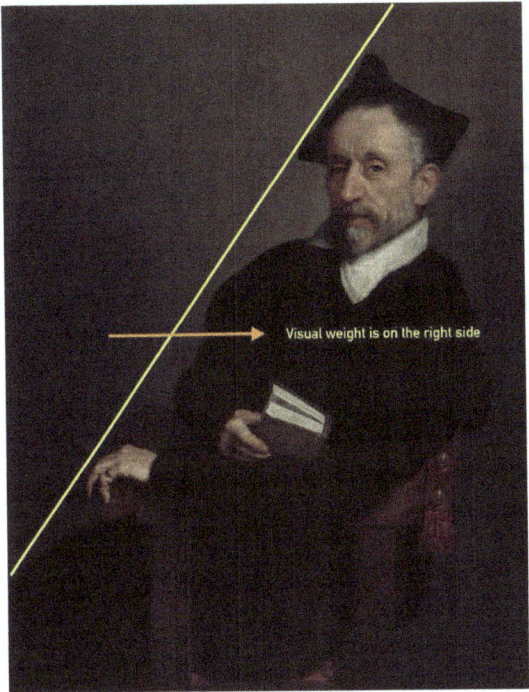

There are exceptions to these concepts, and it's your creative decision to treat their importance. For instance, you can create most of your imagery to the left or right for dramatic effect. You can use this method to direct the eye around your artwork and create a specific narrative as if to say, "Look at this first!"

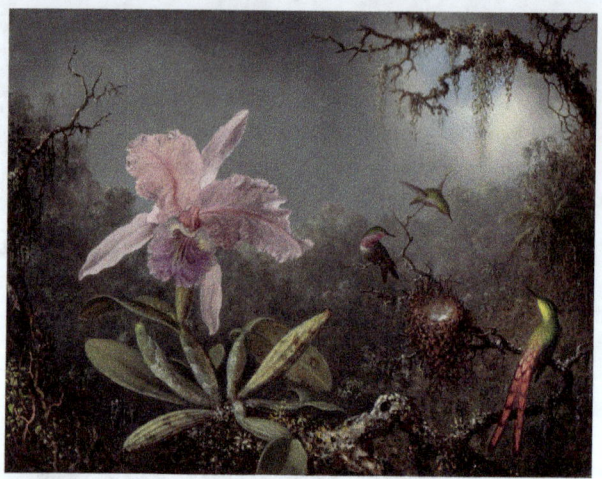

Consider this painting by Martin Johnson Heade. The balance here leads our eyes first toward the pink flower in the foreground and then the birds and trees in the background. Heade uses bright contrast in the foreground to ensure we look there first. The balanced imagery in this painting, even though the pink flower is significant on the left side, is equalized by the tree's branches and the hummingbirds.

[Martin Johnson Heade](#), [Cattleya Orchid and Three Hummingbirds](#)" c.1871 oil on wood.

CREATIVE EXERCISE TO UNDERSTAND TECHNIQUES AND MATERIALS

Here's a quick exercise for understanding techniques and materials. Close your eyes and imagine having pride in yourself for finishing your next piece of art. Describe it to yourself. Imagine everything you'll need to create that piece of art. For example, acrylic paint and a canvas, clay and an oven, and stone and a chisel. This is just a small sample of materials you may need. The array of materials you can use as an artist can go as far as your imagination! Remember, materials and techniques are the backbone of your creative process and may change over time.

VALUE & CONTRAST

For our purposes, value is a scale of color from light to dark in any finished artwork. For example, many different shades exist between stark white and the darkest black, even in a black-and-white image. The lighter shades are called highlights. The darker shades can be called shadows or lowlights. The difference in value between highlights and shadows in an artwork is called contrast. The shape and placement of highlights or shadows give viewers information, such as the direction of a light source or the time of day.

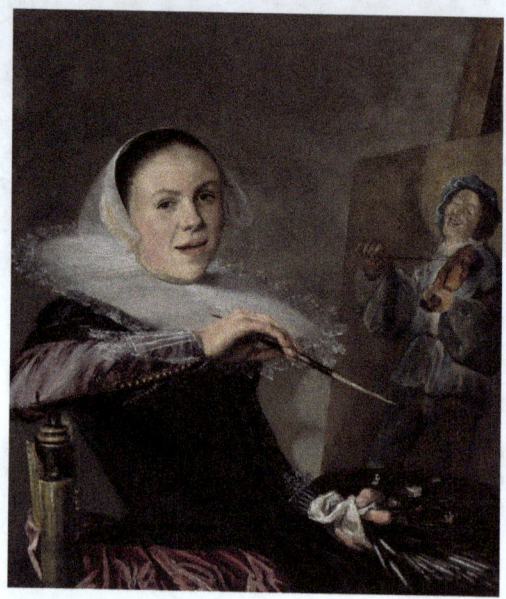

Let's consider this painting from art history. "Self-portrait" was created by Judith Leyster in 1630. The lightest highlights on her face and the darkest shadow distance define the value of this image. The darker values and diminished contrast of the painting within a painting in this image give a sense that it's further back in the frame of view.

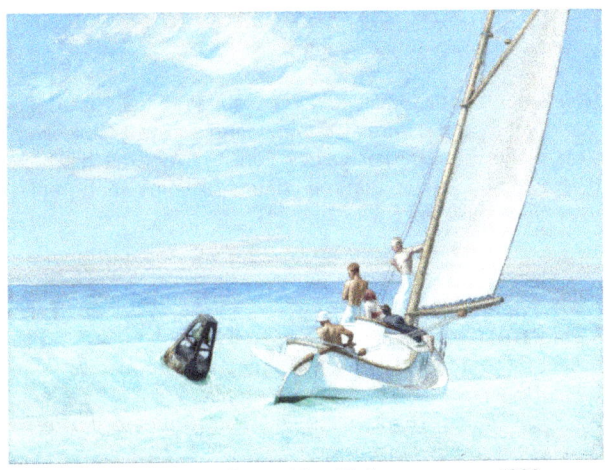

Edward Hopper, "Ground Swell," oil on canvas, c. 1939

Let's also consider this painting from art history to help us understand. Edward Hopper created this painting, and it's called "Ground Swell." This painting portrays bright daytime values. Notice how it has less contrast between the highlight and shadow to represent daylight.

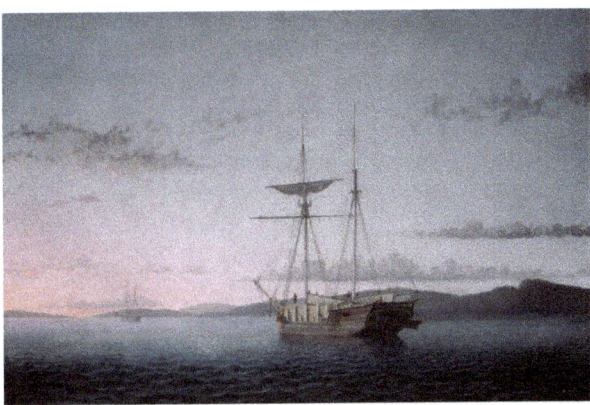

Fitz Henry Lane, "Lumber Schooners at Evening on Penobscot Bay," oil on canvas, c. 1863

Here's another historical painting example to help us understand value and contrast. This painting shows an excellent example of how darker values can help portray dawn or dusk scenery. Notice that the contrast is somewhat greater to achieve this effect.

FORM

The idea of form in painting helps change a two-dimensional object into a three-dimensional one. The form allows us to describe the shape of anything in space. We can use tools like highlighting, shadow, and shading to create the mass and profile of objects in space. The idea of form is quite essential when attempting to paint in a realistic type of style. This element of art helps produce a believable image.

DEPTH

After some experience of painting in acrylic, you will find that your tastes and style may evolve. You may wonder how to advance your work and upgrade your skills. Part of leveling up as a painter is learning new skills and paying attention to detail. The term depth has a few meanings; it can refer to the depth of talent, imagery, or purpose. It may take a little while to grasp, but taking time to add shading to objects will help your work become three-dimensional and pop right off the canvas.

STAGES OF CREATING AN ACRYLIC PAINTING

Understanding the stages of creating an acrylic painting will help demystify the process and help you begin work confidently. It will also help you to comprehend when an image is complete. These are the basic steps you'll take to create a finished acrylic painting. We'll explain what it takes from start to finish and discuss the skills you'll need along the way.

The first step is the sketch. Every painting I've ever created has begun with an illustration. Doing a simple drawing of your idea will help you make sure that the imagery fits on the canvas in a way that's pleasing to the eye. You can also create underpainting by drawing out your sketch using a wash of lighter-colored paint. A wash is an acrylic paint that has been diluted slightly with water. This is the perfect time to ensure that your images are at a good scale and proportionate to one another.

The second step is making your first brush strokes on the canvas. Now it's time to prepare to paint your art. During this step, ensure you have gathered all the basic supplies you'll need for your project. If you want to tone your canvas, now is the time. At this point in your project, it's time to put paint on the canvas. It may seem daunting to take the first step, so take a deep breath and simply start. It's helpful to remember that in acrylic painting, you can wait for the paint to dry and paint over it if you feel you've made a mistake. Take the pressure off yourself by knowing that you can quickly sort out almost anything.

The third is figuring out the details, and this often involves visually studying the subject matter you're painting. This step is the longest part of the painting process and can be one of the best. It includes lots of measuring angles and finding ways to advance the look of your art by adding critical visual cues. Sometimes you can only effectively paint further in your image once you let your paint dry. So, take breaks as often as necessary.

If your colors are mixing on the canvas and looking dull, it's time to take a break.

The next step is about creating the details, highlights, and lowlights. At this point, you'll want to feel confident that you've got every object situated well on the canvas and that everything looks the way you hoped. Some things to consider now are, have I added all the details I wanted? Are the colors bold and bright and match the palette I've chosen? Ensure you've added highlights and lowlights to your painting. It also helps to add depth by using a contour line to set specific imagery to the forefront of the viewer's perspective.

When you feel the painting is complete, sign your work. If you have a title or want to remember the date you finished your art, consider writing something on the back of your canvas or panel.

The final step is finishing your artwork. Finally, when your art has been dry for at least a few days or a week, it's time to consider finishing it. By the finish, we mean adding a varnish to your completed artwork using a spray or applying it with a paintbrush.

I'll let you know how to sketch on a canvas and seal or varnish your painting in subsequent sections of this guidebook.

HOW TO SKETCH ON A CANVAS:

Here are some tips for transferring a drawing to a canvas as this is often the first step toward creating a painting. There are a couple of ways to sketch on a canvas, either freehand or with some assistance from a photo. You can trace directly on your canvas with any pencil. Please note that it's slightly challenging to erase any marks you make, but it's not impossible. Erase using a somewhat light touch so you don't create a tear in the canvas.

To draw on a canvas, you'll need your canvas, a pencil, an eraser, a ruler, and carbon tracing paper.

A grid can help you organize shapes in space as you draw. This technique is helpful when placing subject matter and angles for accurate perspective. Begin by marking one-inch increments across the width of your canvas. Do this on the top and the bottom edges and line each set of markings up with a ruler for straight lines. Remember that it's easier to measure twice and only have to draw the line once correctly. Next, create a line connecting two points at the top and bottom to create vertical lines across your canvas. Repeat this process on the sides of your canvas, going from side to side horizontally. Next, mark one-inch intervals on either side to create precise horizontal lines. Finally, connect two points as you did before across your canvas to create a one-inch grid.

This carbon transfer paper method works to transfer a drawing or printed picture, and it's instrumental if you are new at drawing. Using carbon transfer paper is likely an excellent option for you to try out. It's inexpensive and readily available online and in any art store. Transfer paper comes in various sizes and looks like gray, thin tissue paper. There's going to be a shiny side, which is darker in color, and a dull side, which is lighter and doesn't release carbon. When you use this type of paper, put the shiny side facing your canvas. The carbon from this paper's shiny dark side will transfer onto your canvas's surface when you draw using a pencil on the dull lighter side. To keep the carbon paper in place, you can use a little tape on the back of your canvas. That'll stop it from sliding around.

For this next part, use a drawing you've created or a printed photo of what you want to paint. You can use any image you wish to—tape that in place so it doesn't wiggle around. Next, use a regular pencil and start tracing the things you want to incorporate into the painting. If you're going to leave something out, don't trace it. You will transfer everything you trace via carbon paper to the canvas. These two ways to properly sketch on a canvas are perfectly acceptable. You don't need the grid method if you use carbon paper, but the grid is helpful if you're drawing freehand.

WHEN TO LET PAINT DRY

Letting your paint dry in between layers will help you achieve a boldness of color, which isn't possible when you keep working over wet paint. If too much paint is on the surface of the canvas, it mixes with the previous layer of color. To avoid this, let your paint dry in between layers. Check the label of your paint to see how long it will take to dry; most will say to wait at least 15 minutes. Times may vary, and waiting a bit longer is better than not waiting long enough.

There are a few ways to speed up the drying process of acrylic paint. First, you can use a simple fan pointed at your artwork, which will move the air faster and dry things quickly. Although, beware of a dusty fan or particulates in the air with this method, as wet paint will pick up any pieces of dust in the air. The second way to make your paint dry faster is to mix an additive to it, making it dry quicker between layers. Mix the additive with each color you use per the label instructions and apply as usual.

BASICS OF COLOR

Color is the general term that covers every hue and shade of the light spectrum as we see it with our eyes. The colors red, orange, yellow, green, blue, indigo, and violet, make up the rainbow. So, if you've seen a rainbow, you know what color it is. If color is a general term to describe the entire rainbow, hue is the descriptor for the specific shade. The primary colors are red, yellow, and blue. These colors are primary because it takes no mixing to create them; they are pure pigment. When you mix primary colors, you get a secondary color. You can even create tertiary colors by mixing a secondary color with a primary color. Two examples of tertiary colors are blue-green and yellow-orange.

Some colors need a complement. Each color has a complementary color that is oppositional yet harmonious. Have you ever checked out a color wheel? The color opposite to the color you're using is its complement. For example, red is opposite to green; therefore, they balance and complement one another.

The concept of color and human psychology are inexorably intertwined. Color can influence the feeling of a scene or piece of artwork. As humans, we naturally tend to be influenced by different shades of color. We can all find and make meaning based on the colors presented in art and life. For instance, we use phrases in the English language such as, "I'm feeling blue," and "Green with envy." We can even talk about "seeing red" when meaning to imply that one is feeling angry or very upset. We associate them together, and knowing this is true will help you understand how color can work as a narrative device in your creations over time. Let's consider a bright blue sky during the daytime versus an overcast, gray cloudy sky. The day's atmosphere is the same, but the mood and scenery change drastically.

• HOW TO BLEND COLOR

Blending acrylic paint on a canvas can be daunting until you learn critical skills; there are a few key things to learn to blend acrylics, and this section will help you.

The first way to quickly blend paint while it's on the surface of the canvas is to work while the paint is wet. A wet-on-wet technique implies that the artist continues to paint while the medium is damp; therefore, colors will mix while you paint. If you have ever seen an episode of Bob Ross' Joy of Painting, then you have seen the wet-on-wet painting technique in practice. This technique can cause a muddy or dull color when done incorrectly, though working wet-on-wet can be a skill finessed into working for you.

Another easy way to blend color while it's on the canvas is to work as you usually would and then take a moment to smooth the color out with a dry paintbrush. This simple method can smooth out surfaces and blend color instantly.

Similarly, you can easily blend paint on the canvas using a sponge/sponge brush by combining dots of color while wet. This skill is easy to pick up and will help you create bright swatches of color blended nicely. Another neat way to blend paint is by using a gradient method, which pairs in part with a wet-on-wet technique. To do this, apply strips of color one by one and blend them at the seams while the paint is damp. Clean the brush between color applications if you fear your pigment will become muddy.

HOW TO KEEP COLOR BRIGHT

Let's talk about how to make acrylic paint vibrant, including tips on avoiding muddy colors in acrylic painting. Keeping your paint bright is essential as it can help improve the way your artwork looks from a distance. Dull or muddy color doesn't read as well from afar and can diminish the look of your painting. In addition, accidental over-mixing of colors occurs for a few easily fixable reasons.

When the artist doesn't allow enough time for a layer of paint to dry, the paint begins to blend on the canvas and dims the color you're attempting to use. To keep paint bright, account for drying time and take a break every so often to let your work dry. Allowing dry time will help immensely. Patience is critical here; remember that acrylic paint dry times are relatively quick compared to oil paint! Another big tip to keep your painting bright is to change your paintbrush to water often. Just think, changing the brush cleaning water would be wise if you're painting a big blue sky and want to use crisp white for your clouds. If the water is blue with paint, it will affect your ability to keep your brush clean when you want to paint with crisp white. To avoid unintentional cross-tinting, keep the water in your jar clear by changing it often. This tiny improvement will help keep your paint bright.

TONING THE CANVAS TO INFLUENCE COLOR

Toning your canvas is something you do in the beginning stages of an artwork. To tone a canvas, apply a specific color as the first layer on your canvas. This step allows a chosen hue to shine brighter and influence subsequent layers as you continue working. Toning a painting can be done in varying shades and general shapes of your subject matter. Or, you can choose one color across the entirety of the canvas.

To tone a canvas, you must consider what color you'd like to influence your painting. For instance, if you want to create underwater artwork, you would probably tone the canvas with blue to make it bold. In this instance, you would hypothetically paint a layer of blue first, focusing on where the water would be to maintain brightness. On the other hand, if you were painting a sunset, perhaps the area of the sun would be toned in a bright yellow so that the site would remain the most brilliant part of the art as you work.

It is optional to tone your canvas when painting any subject, but it is a way to finesse the brightness of color for your artwork. You can have a successful painting without specifically toning the canvas, but it can be beneficial in some instances. For example, if you're looking for a good and bold effect of color, toning your canvas may help you do that.

• MOST USED COLORS TO PURCHASE

With time, you may realize that you use specific paint colors more frequently than others. The paints you use up faster will depend on what you like to paint. For instance, if you love painting hilly landscapes, you may run out of green shades faster. On the other hand, if you adore painting seascapes, you may need more blue shades than different colors. That said, I'd like to give you an idea of the primary colors you'll need to get started and what you are likely to purchase more frequently.

As a beginner, it may be wise to begin with a starter set of paints to get used to this new medium. The kits I'm referring to include essential items like paintbrushes and small tubes of color in varying shades. In the kit, you will find black and white, two shades of red, orange, two types of yellow, light and dark green, blue, and brown. Each tube in these sets tends to be relatively small and won't carry you through more than two paintings, depending on the surface size used. But it can give you a good idea of how long the paint lasts and what colors you might like to use in the future. These kits are pretty affordable, too! In my practice, I tend to bulk up on black and white paint as it seems to disappear faster than other shades. As a person who loves landscape and seascape paintings, I often find myself running out of leaf green and brown. Blues seem to disappear quickly as well.

My method of keeping the necessary colors around is a simple mental inventory. Or, if there's a sale at Michael's or insert-your-local-art-store here, then it may be worth your time to look over what you've got and what you might need. Taking advantage of sales is something I love to do, and it's helped me trim my painting budget. Also, it is helpful to sign up for any rewards or loyalty programs offered. For instance, you can rack up points towards $5.00 product vouchers at Michael's and use them on just about anything. If you get their app, you can instantly surf their inventory, be notified of upcoming and current sales, and find coupons. I also love that you can order and pick it up in store for free! You can't beat that.

● COLOR MAP MASTER LIST

The following section will be beneficial if you want to learn how to mix your shades on the fly. Follow my color mixing equations below and use this list as a reference when you're in the midst of a project. Regarding the vernacular I use in this list, a 'part' can be any amount of paint suitable for your needs. The only thing to remember is to keep your volumes similar. Whatever you decide a 'part' is, keep it consistent.

Consider a few helpful things as you learn to mix color. First, do you need something to be lighter than what you mixed? Add small amounts of white to your mix and incorporate it well until the color is light enough. Add a small amount of black or brown and mix your color well if you need a darker shade. In some situations, you might lighten a color with a bright shade, such as yellow, or deepen a shade by adding a darker hue, like brown or blue. Color is situational; you will feel more comfortable mixing colors as you spend more time painting.

Reds:

Bright Reddish Pink: Medium pink, a dash of orange and red.

Light Pink: Lots of white, a small amount of red.

Medium Pink: 1 part red, 2-3 parts white.

Deep red: Lots of red, a dash of dark brown or black.

Red-Orange: 3 parts red, 1 part yellow.

Terra Cotta: 1 part red, 1 part yellow ochre, and a dash of brown.

Orange Shades:

Medium orange: Equal parts yellow and red.

Light orange or Yellow Orange: 3-4 parts yellow, 1 part red.

Burnt Orange: Equal parts yellow and red with a dash of dark brown.

Yellow Shades

Yellow Orange: Lots of yellow and a dash of red.

Burnt Yellow: Lots of yellow and a touch of brown; add white if you need this color lighter.

Green Shades:

Leaf Green: 1 part blue, two parts yellow.

Light Green: 1 part blue, 2-3 parts yellow.

Dark Green: Equal parts blue and yellow; add a dash of brown or black, depending on how deep you want the color to be.

Blue Shades

Night Sky Blue (very dark): 3 parts blue, 1 part black, perhaps more depending on your needs.

Sky blue: Lots of white and a dash of medium (royal) blue.

Periwinkle blue: Lots of white, 1 part blue, and a bit of red.

Blue-green/turquoise: 2 parts blue, 1 part green.

Aqua: 2 parts blue, 1 part green, 1 part white.

Purple: 2 parts red, 1 part blue.

Light Purple/Pink: Add dashes of red and blue to white or a touch of purple to a light pink mixture.

Magenta: Start with mostly red, a dash of blue, and a small amount of orange.

Deep Purple: 2 parts blue, 1 part red, a dash of black or more depending on how dark you'd like this to be.

Gray: 2 parts white, 1 part black to start. Add more white or black to shift shades.

Tan: Mix primarily white with a dash of brown and yellow.

• COLOR PALETTE

In painting, every color you use in the given artwork constitutes your palette of colors. Some colors look nice together; this idea of "excellent" will vary widely amongst individuals. Monotone means the palette is limited in shades and hues, like a theme based on one color. A high contrast palette means a big difference between the lightest and darkest colors, creating a wide range of values. For example, your palette could consist of sepia colors or be black-and-white, including all shades of gray in between.

It is your choice to design this group before you begin to work. Keep track as you go or record this information after completing the piece. There are several reasons to choose colors beforehand. These include operating to the standard of a client or commission, making artwork for matching home decor, or creating a series of works with similar colors. Reasons for recording your chosen color palette may include sharing your process with friends or online, remembering the choices made for a future similar piece, or recording your progress.

HOW TO SAVE YOUR PAINT FROM DRYING OUT

Once you get into a good practice of painting several times a week, you'll come up against a few problems to solve. One of those items that many people express incredible frustration with is paint drying out quickly. Drying out may happen because you've been working a while, and your color ends up drying on your palette before you've got a chance to use it, which can be annoying! It may also happen by accident between painting sessions where the canvas needs to dry, but your paint needs to remain pliable. It's also possible that one might forget to cover up their paint. In any of these cases, once the paint is dry, it cannot be returned. It's a wasted product.

Thankfully, there are tons of ways to save your paint between sessions and even between painting projects. There are fancier ways to do this and many DIY options with household items.

My favorite style of paint palette is called a "[Sta-Wet Handy Palette](#)," which has a lining that helps your paint retain its moisture over time. It also comes with a tightly fitting lid that allows the color to last much longer. These palettes are affordable and could be a fine choice for many. The technology is simplistic yet helpful, and you can extend the life of your paint to weeks!

If you have the wooden or plastic palette that came with your beginner paint set, don't fret because there are options for you too! In this case, you can wrap your palette with cling film/plastic wrap all the way around to retain moisture. Beware of wrapping too tightly and possibly smooshing the small piles of paint you may have mixed. Another way to save the color on these palettes is to put the entire thing into a large zipper-style plastic bag. This method allows you to keep the paint longer than you imagine. If you open the bag and notice a mildew smell, the color has been sitting for too long.

There are also good options to save paint affordably by using plastic paint pots. You can find this style of paint container at your local art supply store. Sometimes, even the dollar store will have these little containers. Each of these small jars has a rubberized lid to keep the canister airtight, allowing another use of that paint. These are especially helpful when you have mixed a specific shade and want to keep the same mixture for the entirety of your painting project. You can also use these to separate highlight, middle tone, and shadow shades in the same color for portraits of people or pets. Mixing paint for a project in this way can potentially save you time and hassle as you continue to work. Also, this method will help you keep your colors consistent and bright.

Another DIY method for saving paint utilizes products you may have lying around your home. For example, if you have an extra ice cube tray or several in your home, you have a strangely fabulous palette right in front of you! Each well is much deeper than traditional paint palettes, and they stack impeccably well for storage on any shelf. To save paint using this method, wrap the entire thing in plastic or use that marvelously self-adhesive cling film that sticks wherever you press. The third idea is to put the whole thing into a large freezer zipper bag; the bags I use can fit a couple of ice tray palettes. This method is convenient when working on multiple projects with varying color palettes.

HOW TO ADD HIGHLIGHT AND SHADOW, LIGHT SOURCE

Several factors work together in a painting to make things seem three-dimensional and believable. Understanding how light affects the look of any object is imperative when adding highlight and shadow. Adding light and shadow creates form in space. Light from the left side of the frame affects things differently than light from above. The same is true for light shining from the right side or glowing from below.

When light is very bright or firm, it will increase the contrast between the lightest and darkest values contained in any given object. As a painter, it'll be helpful for you to remember that skin tone will use at least three shades of color to portray light in your artwork. It may be that you will use some more colors than just three shades. But three is a good start; these three tones include the brightest highlights, middle style, and shadow color. Even if the light source is diffused or dimmer, please use three shades at least.

HOW TO MEASURE & PAINT ANYTHING

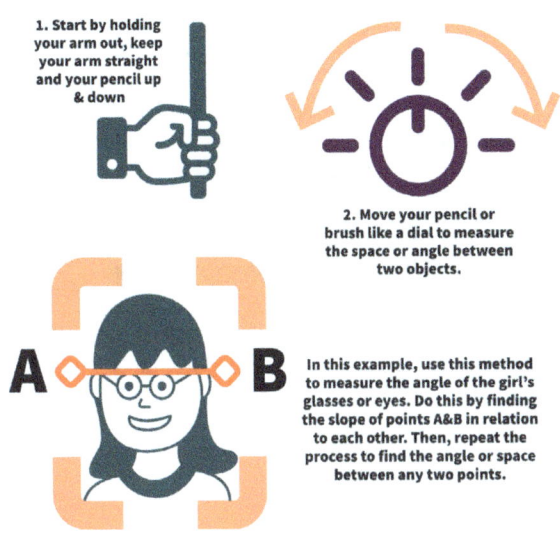

1. Start by holding your arm out, keep your arm straight and your pencil up & down

2. Move your pencil or brush like a dial to measure the space or angle between two objects.

In this example, use this method to measure the angle of the girl's glasses or eyes. Do this by finding the slope of points A&B in relation to each other. Then, repeat the process to find the angle or space between any two points.

This section will teach you one easy technique to help you measure and paint anything.

This necessary skill helped me immensely in art school and beyond. It will undoubtedly help you have the confidence to paint any subject matter over time and is a way to check your accuracy while working. I'm happy to share it with you because I know it will transform your skills.

All you'll need to practice this skill is a paintbrush or a pencil.

Get out your paintbrush or pencil, and visualize being in front of your easel or canvas. Picture your chosen subject matter in front of you. Where do you even begin? The thing about measuring is that it does take a little bit of patience. However, this skill, as simple as it may be, will help you paint anything. It's straightforward—hold your arm straight out to measure the angle while using your paintbrush as a dial. Make marks on the canvas when you measure. You must keep a straight arm to ensure accuracy. Next, hold your paintbrush or pencil up and down; move it like a dial as you measure angles. For instance, if you're painting a face, you may want to measure the tip of their eyes to other facial features. In the example above, use this method to measure the angle of the girl's glasses or eyes. Do this by finding the slope of points A and B in relation to each other. Then, repeat the process to find the angle or space between any two points.

TIPS FOR PAINTING FINE DETAILS

There will come a point in any painting where you want to focus the imagery and provide the necessary detail to create accuracy. So, let's discuss some essential tips for painting fine detail in acrylic. My first piece of advice is to use detailer brushes. Tiny brushes are the master key to creating little details and small embellishments, enhancing the look of your artwork.

The second important thing to do is study your subject matter closely. It takes some critical thought to further the look of your painting. You must be able to look at the item you're painting and then at your art in its current state to figure out which details may be missing. Take your time and have patience as you study the intricacies of your subject matter and artwork. Finally, write down the items you want to fix or enhance to keep your thoughts in order. You'll be glad you wrote these items down when you begin your next painting session.

Tip number three is to consider all the highlights and shadows. Factors like these can help define the shape of things, giving your art depth of imagery. These additions will instantly level up the look of your work. Next, consider if the shadows and highlights you've created make sense with the light's direction. Keep your highlights and shadows consistent according to that information, and you'll be well on your way to a detailed painting.

Tip number four involves measuring angles, proportions, and scale. By taking the time to assess angles, balance, and scale, you'll quickly improve the accuracy of your artwork. To complete this task, measure things often using your paintbrush, even if this means moving things around a bit. Again, use the skill you learned in the previous section to help you complete this necessary task.

Tip number five is to consider texture. The texture is the surface of an object that light reveals. Consider the texture of what you're painting and the use of detailer brushes to add these essential visual cues to your artwork. With these tips in mind, you'll be able to create fine details in your painting.

HOW TO REMOVE EXCESS PAINT

There are easy ways to fix excess acrylic paint on your canvas or painting surface. You can do a few different things to get the leftover paint off the canvas. For example, if you have just created an acrylic pour painting and want to start over and get all the color off, we recommend using a pallet knife to scrape the excess off your canvas. Using a larger pallet knife will do this job quicker, but any size will do. Scrape the canvas but don't apply too much pressure to preserve the canvas' surface. Avoid tearing a hold in your surface, which would render it unusable.

If you have a little goof up and want to 'erase' what you just did, you can usually go in with a clean damp paintbrush and work at the paint until it comes off the canvas. But, of course, this only works when the paint is still wet, so act quickly.

If you have a large area of your painting that you'd like to change but the paint has dried, then you must paint over what you already have. Ensure the paint is completely dry before you do this to avoid muddying the color on your canvas. Take a deep breath and begin again.

HOW TO VARNISH AN ACRYLIC PAINTING

Varnishing a painting protects it for years to come. This simple step allows the artwork to retain its colorful brightness over time and protects your artwork from dirt and dust, which makes it easier to clean. With this step, the artist creates a beautiful veneer and a layer of protection for the future. This section will teach you how to varnish acrylic paintings with spray and how to brush varnish. Keep in mind that there are several types of finishes regarding varnish. When we mention the finish, it's about how shiny or dull the result is. Several finishes are available, ranging from no sheen to extremely shiny, starting with matte, satin, gloss, and high gloss.

To varnish an acrylic painting, you'll need these materials:

1. If brush varnishing; a clean glass jar for varnish and a large flat brush

2. A mask and a well-ventilated area to work in

3. Apron and gloves

To spray varnish your art, take your thoroughly dried and cured painting to a well-ventilated space, such as outdoors. Even outdoors, please use a respirator mask as spray varnish is very potent. Cover the area you're working in with plastic sheeting, a trash bag, or paper to protect the surface. Lay your artwork flat and test your spray varnish for clogs by spraying short bursts away from your painting before you begin. Spray using side-to-side motions at least 12"-18" away from your art. Please note: several light layers of this varnish are better than over-spraying once. Use a light touch while doing this step and repeat light layers once the previous layer has dried. Pay attention to the label; you may need to layer varnish a few times, but let it all dry between applications.

If you want to brush and varnish your art, you'll need a few things besides a good mask, an apron, and a well-ventilated work area. First, ensure a clean glass jar (or cup) and a large dry paintbrush. Next, carefully pour varnish into the jar; try to avoid bubbles as you do this. If bubbles are in the varnish, eliminate them by using your brush to move them against the inner sides of the jar. Next, carefully apply varnish using even side-to-side brush strokes. Be aware of any bubbles or bristles that might get caught in the finish. Remove any imperfections before the varnish dries.

Once you're varnished, the painting is complete. It's not wise to paint on top of varnish as it will negatively affect any added paint over time. Also, please let your newly-varnished work dry completely before storing your art. If you store your art before it's ready, it may stick to surfaces that would cause superficial damage. Check the varnish label to find out the exact dry time for the product you're using.

HOW TO STORE YOUR CANVAS

The best environment for canvas storage and canvas painting storage is a place that doesn't have direct sunlight, wild temperature changes, or moisture. A canvas panel painting should be stored only when it has had a chance to dry thoroughly. The most accessible canvas storage on a dime is to wrap your art up in wax or parchment paper and place them gently into a banker's box or any box with a top. In actuality, you can use whatever you'd like for canvas painting storage, but please remember to use a material that won't stick to your paintings. If something sticks to your artwork, it may pull the paint off when you unwrap it. Also, remember not to pack your images too tightly so that the surface of your work isn't affected.

WAYS TO CHANGE THE NATURE OF ACRYLIC PAINT USING ADDITIVES

You can add a medium to acrylic paint to alter its physical properties. Mediums usually come in the form of a see-through gel or liquid. They may exist in tubes, jars, or jugs. The consistency of these mediums is very similar to paint, and it helps to be mindful of the finish. Each additive has its finish, which will affect the paint you're using. Like varnish, gel medium is available in many levels of shine. The dullest finish with no sheen is called matte; satin has very little shine but isn't dull, gloss is moderately shiny, and a high gloss finish adds lots of shine.

These additives can do a myriad of things for your artwork. Mediums are very useful as they allow us to alter the various properties of acrylic paint. When working with acrylic paints, gels and mediums are incorporated into your color to change its normal behavior.

Some mediums help with acrylic pouring, too. There are even mediums that bulk up your paint and make it a thick paste, as is desirable in impasto painting. As a reminder, impasto painting implies that the color is very thick and textured, leaving a raised surface to your artwork.

There are also mediums available that will slow them from drying too quickly. Typically, these mediums will be labeled 'slow dry' or retardant. Slowing your paint down from drying too fast is an exciting feature of painting as it allows you to blend your colors easier if they take longer to dry, which may help portrait painters. Also, a longer dry time enables you to render skin smoothly by having more time to blend skin tones. A medium like this will assist you in blending any gradients or smoothing out brush marks left over from your paint brushes.

HOW TO JOIN ACRYLIC ARTS ACADEMY'S HELPFUL ARTIST COMMUNITIES

At Acrylic Arts Academy, we offer two helpful Facebook communities to teach and encourage you on your painting journey. These communities are called "Acrylic Painting Tutorials for Beginners and Beyond" and the "Artist Promotion Group."

Find & join our groups here: https://www.facebook.com/AcrylicArtsAcademy/groups

Members of our groups feel supported, encouraged, and they improve their skills week after week. They learn new techniques and best practices while finding inspiration.

Here's how to use this group:

First, please read the rules of our group as they are essential to follow. This group consists of both students and teachers.

You'll see acrylic painting tutorials from Acrylic Arts Academy and many other talented teachers worldwide. Some will show up as YouTube links; when you click those, you'll be redirected to YouTube on your device to view the rest of the video. If you enjoy the video, hit the thumbs-up button on Facebook to let us and the other teachers know which videos you enjoy the most.

If the video begins to play while you're scrolling through our group's feed, it just means that the creator has uploaded that content directly to Facebook, and you can view it there. You are welcome to leave a comment on any video, especially if you have a question or need clarification on a technique/skill. If you like the tutorial you see so much that you want to share it with your friends, you're always welcome to share your favorite posts from our group on your profile.

At the top, you'll find our banner image and the group's name. There's also information about how many group members are with us. In this area, several horizontally listed "tabs" are in bold lettering. These are the most important items for new community members to see and can help you start painting. You can easily find our daily posts from our channel in the "Featured" section. We welcome you to leave comments to let us know what you like about each tutorial or ask for clarification on techniques. We answer posts at least three times a day. If you find that your post or comment was not approved, then please be patient. We will get to your request within 24 hours. If you have a question about acrylic painting or one of our tutorials, we welcome you to ask us in a post in this group. We will happily give answers and explain anything you may need to know.

If you want to post a picture of your artwork to share with peers, please join our Artist Promotion Group. The Artist Promotion Group is a positive and helpful place to share your artwork with other artist peers. Ask us for help or tips to advance any painting, and you'll find that many people will answer you and support your creative journey. People find this group to be a positive, welcoming, and constructive place.

Members of our Artist Promotion Group report feeling inspired, share reference photos, learn from examples from art history, and discuss art. This group paints specific monthly themes that inspire you while being helped by fellow artists. Artists in his community are supported as they have a place to ask questions. Some members sell their art in their local communities, gain commissions, and learn best practices for being professional artists.

Wherever you are in your painting journey, Acrylic Arts Academy's online communities can support your practice. Join either of our communities on Facebook by following the links in the description below. Or, just log onto Facebook and search for us.

We look forward to seeing you in these groups. Thanks for reading this guidebook, and we'll see you next time!

www.ingramcontent.com/pod-product-compliance
Lightning Source LLC
Chambersburg PA
CBHW050255220526
45465CB00002B/693